The Fields

Richard Silberg

Pennywhistle Press

Malibu & San Francisco

1989

Cover photograph by Margaret Wright
Design/typesetting by Susan Galleymore
Cover design by The Groot Organization, San Francisco

Printed in the United States of America
        by The Watermark Press, San Francisco

ISBN 0-938631-05-5

For additional copies, address orders to: Pennywhistle Press
                                            2637 Hyde Street
                                            San Francisco, CA 94109

Contents

INTRODUCTION BY JOYCE JENKINS — iv

THE CENTER — 7
THE 60's — 8
THE WORD — 9
EACH'S OWN — 10
POSTMODERN — 11
WILD CATS AND WEEDS — 12
THE LARGER TIME — 13
I, TOO, DISLIKE IT… — 14
GENESIS OF AN ATHEIST — 15
CATHEDRAL 3 — 16
LEOPARD MAN — 17
LEOPARD MAN II — 18
PEARLDIVER'S PALIMPSEST — 19
THE HOPEFUL HORSE — 20
FIRST THINGS — 21
POETRY AND REAL ESTATE: AT CODY'S CAFE — 22
THE FIELDS — 24
MASSING — 26
TURNOVER — 27
OUR VISIT TO BODIE — 29
BACKWARDS — 30
OUTSIDE ELI'S — 31

Introduction

Richard Silberg is a New Yorker. He is a critic, an actor, and currently, a teacher at UC Extension in Berkeley. As a younger man, before his life as a poet, he was a self-styled prophet spinning theories in *The Devolution of the People*, which was published by a New York house in 1967. He is also my friend, my colleague, my right arm and left lobe at *Poetry Flash*, the San Francisco Bay Area's Poetry Review and Literary Calendar, of which I am editor and publisher.

Richard is a maverick of American poetry—perhaps in the sense of Steve Kowit's recent anthology, *The Maverick Poets*. The dictionary definitions of "maverick" include: one who refuses to abide by the dictates of the group, a dissenter, one who resists adherence to or affiliation with any single organized group or faction; an independent. No poet is more independent than Richard Silberg, yet he is the perfect 'star foil,' (my play on his *Translucent Gears* poem, "Star Fur,"), known to many unfamiliar with the poetry or literary 'scene' only as that kind of a presence, hosting bookparties at Cody's Books in Berkeley, where he has also coordinated the poetry series for some years.

Richard Silberg's shrewd, short reviews, written since 1984 for *Poetry Flash* under the "New & Noted" rubric, bear his definitive critical style. In fact, their compressed language, with all superfluous baggage removed—new words invented from the old—crunch more meaning into less space than the work of almost any other reviewer or critic.

Like the wildly differing Majorie Perloff or Tom Clark, Silberg can be piercing, but the hallmark of his style, besides the new, metaphoric use of language, and crunch snap of his observations, is not slash and burn. He doesn't suffer fools *gladly*, but he does sometimes, with compassion, suffer them, and he never reviews anything that he cannot in some way respect, grant its due. He has the kind of integrity which won't let him touch translations if he doesn't have at least a reading knowledge of the original languages (French, German, Roumanian, Spanish), and the original texts of the poems handy.

His critical style, loaded with "1 em" dashes—those free-standing twists of phrase—is also basic to *The Fields*. Representative of the best of his shorter work from recent years, these staccato little pieces stand in firm contrast to the longer, almost story-like poems we have seen from him in the past.

What you have in your hands in *The Fields* are short poems, the condensed version, the skinny of this wise and twinkly man's work. He is, in these poems, compelling the language itself to take a step, in much the same way that his long poems step in from his novel, and his short "New & Noted" reviews step in from his longer pieces. These short poems are small slits cut in the canvas which wraps us, which, when the eye is held against them, ray out and open up a whole world on the other side.

The compression inherent in these poems makes them necessarily more abstract than the poet's longer poems, and the tone is often lighter, even in "First Things," with its memories of childhood. They are shinier, sometimes glittering like coal pressed in a Superman's hand—quick observations, snapshots taken with a poet's eye ("Turnover" and "Our Visit to Bodie"). More restless than his longer poems, they travel with Richard on his average day, see out of his eyes—and note what they see in a shorthand which is his own.

They are as complete, mysterious, and whole unto themselves as one leopard-like, solitary, but not lonely, man working every day, on schedule, at his craft. Over and over, these poems depict the dream of writing, the imagery of writing, with the cats and sparrows in their "pearly entropy" as "he worked peaceful/ as an ox in Heaven," the word dancing in sunlight.

Joyce Jenkins
Berkeley, CA
August 1, 1989

THE CENTER

Drinking coffee on the boulevard
with Carroll the astrologer
and Sal
    returned from long ago
talking Seattle Hawaii
settlements of people we knew
the shine of their eyes
over time and space

    I remembered
a pollenburst of chickadees
in the air rising to the Berkeley hills
catapult into space
the trees breathing
across the crest
like a tremendous pelt

not to need
shelter and center
These eaves are the heavens
This floor our plowed fields
This hearth our wedded love
to be beyond
        flesh
        and nostalgia
    in the pure sunlight

THE 60's

Some of them are dead now
Time stands
dividing angel
But things were opening
to us then
they were
really opening
Jittering spider light
black coffee
over our heads
in eye corners
the cloudy pearls were opening

THE WORD

He had a
shy chewed up face
drinker ruddy
and losing hair
Told me
after my reading
about teaching at Soledad
how he'd read "Howl"
to those cats
thieves rapists murderers
how quiet they were
pin drop
appreciative grateful
"lambs to the word"
I'd been wandering on the page
a sky
blindness
all messages stopped
Four generations of photographs
on his wall
great-great to his parents
marriages
Southern faces
"Lambs to the word"
he said
and brought me back

EACH'S OWN

a crumbling breastwork   and
lo came lumbering
words in weariness
as in that other poem   you
know   stumbling on crutches past
hospital beds   towards love's
disappearing door

POSTMODERN

swimming here
in the trough of what
's got to be a wave

WILD CATS AND WEEDS

re: poetry as music
it's not abstract
there's a catness to the sound

THE LARGER TIME

Only senses
Not this and this
my half-face cat
calico and black
bare winter persimmon
filled with sparrows
Not the rose bush
sawn at the root
invisible roses
unknuckling   glistening
Not one of these
but many
multiplied
voices   lights
whistling and streaming

I, TOO, DISLIKE IT...

the sea crests
around a bend
beyond poetry's
validation and
seen by other heads
other heads
speak to me and we
       suck
   tongues
weave the tongues
and taste the
pearly entropy

GENESIS OF AN ATHEIST

He was a kind
of gray Santa Claus
diffident and blurry
I dreamed him one night
for the first
and last time
As if through a screen door
he spoke to me
but I don't
remember what he said
"You piss me off"?
or was it a secret
like
the true name for 'bird'
like
an emblem of things?
Anyway
some transfer
some spark
And when I woke
God wasn't inside
or outside
He wasn't
anywhere at all

CATHEDRAL 3

He dreamed of working
everlasting stone
It billowed
upbubbling
quirky shapes
sphinxes manticores demons
saints angels
Mary Christ
The stone breathed
slowly
registered and held
the slightest chisel stroke
His hands chewed their stony cuds
and he worked peaceful
as an ox in Heaven

LEOPARD MAN

The muscular
curves of my legs are writing
a dream of writing
as if you felt
a story could arise
jungle path
that snakes toward a waiting
tree
stone fruit
the death
written on dream paper

LEOPARD MAN II

Once they were the tribal
terror police
White leopard fire
purred
in moving many-pointed darkness
Once they lay down in a gash
in the earth like a cunt
The witch doctor rode them
masked
fang face
and carved the secret
in their backs
If they screamed
they died
and if they were silent
leopardlike
they rose with curved claws

Now when they stalk
they shine
They are the secret itself
the carving itself
the crystal thread
that runs through sleep

PEARLDIVER'S PALIMPSEST

I was working swingshift
not sleeping enough
awake in a dream
Writing in coffeehouses
my mind would drift
I found myself hearing
the voices at once
the one big voice
barbarbarbarbarbar
progenitive
deep lurking
sea sound
Washing the pots
I'd work through shapes
food stains creeping
eyes hands claws
down to clean metal
the scratches and tarnish
as if that were truth
I got closer and closer

THE HOPEFUL HORSE

Yes
I'm a hypochondriac
but hypochondriacs
have real diseases
Arrested in monkish emptiness
I'm charged with light
and sentenced to bright hell
As a young man I wrung
passion from my situation
now
now I ride it
flogging the hopeful horse

FIRST THINGS

A tooth tingling weewee
or some four year old ur-orgasm
as if I died and
came back again
pressed against the swampy globe
But the globe was Aunt Sadie's girdle
enormous   with a window in it
and she   a raucous Bronx woman
one generation out of Vilna
who wore her stockings
rolled on dumpling white legs
was riding
a red rhinoceros

     long
radius from childhood
I remember this
forty six years old
sliding sideways
in the flesh

POETRY AND REAL ESTATE:
AT CODY'S CAFE

for Jerry Ratch

"Selling real estate
is like hunting.
It's OK.
After so long, I
know what I'm doing."
His gaze is even
but as if something is constricting
his insides
"Money. When you do business
with people, then you know them."
Across from us
the burned out hotel
glows   Washed
cloudy sunlight after rain
deepens the greens and reds
organ red of brick
a heavy stubborn color
empty gutted windows
"And then I pry time
for the poetry.
This new book
is good. Really good.
But I can't tell you how hard
the writing was."
Long look   Almost
imploring
"Indescribably hard.
As if I aged five years
to shape it get
something clear
from the murk.
I felt all my grey hairs
sprouting."

He looks at me
in the rainy light
A hungry hollow
As if the poetry
is hunting him

THE FIELDS

As I read
the dream bloomed
and I entered it
He was speaking
"matters of grace"
anastomosing anti-worlds
He evoked
the common dream
so that we were
facets of the zeitgeist
sleepwalkers
puppets but
we could follow our strings
our fracture lines
back into the glow

Gratefully I told him my own
dream visions
climbing through rotten museums
The mortuary dream in which
the lovers mix delicately
as liquids in the grave
Peter's explanations
the dry cerements
lightning hit the evidential pot
The Black girl and Mendelssohn
his music a rustling of angels
Was her angry cry
the world regained?
the angels lost?
the story with its veins popped out
a bum rummaging through
subway trash
"I got to find me some M&M's...
something that will keep..."
a free man in the nickel package

I spoke these things
to his picture on the back book flap
but
his reaction wasn't personal
He nodded
as if remembering
and just absorbed what I'd said
to further talk
and further writing
How lonely it was then
annihilating
We couldn't mingle
our dreams
We were like
parallel lines
horses grazing past each other
in the fields of intertextuality

MASSING

They were a mother and daughter act
at the poetry readings
both dark
hair and skin
pressed to the limits
of respectability
the little girl aggressive
gypsyish
wanting and posing
coquette   coquette
Now here she is
the mother
parading the avenue alone
in an army jacket
and she's flipped
slipped through
And how do I know this?
The army jacket?
Her furtive vague-eyed walk?
Her face is subtly different
puffy   thickened
like a glove
It seems yellower   Can
that be?   reddish
in its creases
And behind her glovelike
masklike face
it's as though she's lolling
open   sucking on herself
Something obscene   huge and sly
Artaud mountains there   the Momo
his body a black turd
sizzled by electricity
sizzled black in hospital bowels
slick terrifying shit
massing at the hole

TURNOVER

She got on at 21st and Broadway
the sweltering heart
fantasmagoric hooker
in a platinum blond wig
shaggy white fake fur coat
80° in downtown Oakland
and this slim black lady
seemed cool
lacquered and tinkling and almost kabuki
zombied out and demon dead
Seven blocks to 14th and Broadway
        I forgot her
droning   crowded dream
of breath and sweat
But getting out
I saw a teen-age black kid
shove her through the door
yell something
did she hassle him?
hit on him?
Then as I stepped out the door myself
she shook off her polar bear coat
like lightning
stark naked
at the bus stop
in a crowded ring
pointing and shrieking
fork-eyed   fanged
she hurled her
honey brown cleft body
at the kid
like shrapnel
scraggly small curves and her bush
ripped off her wig
and she was shaven bald
Three cop cars rayed in

on the bus out of nowhere
as I left
Two hours turning
in the downtown gear teeth
I catch the bus to Berkeley
drone past
21st and Broadway
There she is
hanging in the traffic
beyond belief
paid for by whom?
Two hours
bared
busted and booked
and she's on the set again
malicious small pagoda
in her jewelry   coat   wig

OUR VISIT TO BODIE

(a burned out California goldmining town)

Clean wooden ship shape church
sailing the wide black fire scar
refining machinery on the hill
saloons and stores and shacks
all deserted
Bodie
echo
of American self-sufficiency
courage   hard work
and greed
shrunk to the personal
blackened crisp
of our sex and tenderness
your hatchet head floating
among the ghost lost
shafts and wheels

BACKWARDS

Sadness of the slip knot
sliding the same bad
faith poem
"Nothing that the light says
will save you"
Saved or damned it's
the same pomposity
Remember
in kindergarten
we planted lima beans
in milk cartons
and you were
strewn shining?
The sprout humped out
backwards
and left the bean behind

OUTSIDE ELI'S

They've broken into my car
I'm standing around the corner
from Eli's Mile High Club
Night of the blues   spangled glass
Claudia's left for Hawaii
(with a good man at last)
who I first saw on Telegraph Avenue
in 1966
looking like Sheena of the Jungle
who I last made love to on my 37th
birthday   when I was exactly
half my father's age
Like the blues
like Eli's
Claudia unites the black and the white
in sweetness
and pain
in her son Orlando's golden afro
Long flowering stem
of my seedtime
The sixties are gone
Somewhere
far away
the lion lies down with the lamb
They're fucking
Everything gleams
There's a spangled hole
where my right rear window
used to be